HENRY

story by F. R. Robinson
illustrations by Larry Moore

HARCOURT BRACE & COMPANY

Orlando Atlanta Austin Boston San Francisco Chicago Dallas New York
Toronto London

Henry wasn't like his brothers and sisters.

He had a large beak.
They didn't.

He had feathers.
They didn't.
"Oh, Henry!
Please clean up
after yourself!"
said Mother Lizard.

Henry had two long legs and big toes.
They had four short legs and small toes.

Mother Lizard smiled and said,
"Come here my beautiful babies.
Henry, the time has come.
You must go to school."

"Why?" asked Henry.
"Because you are special,"
she said. "You have wings.
You must learn to use them."

At first nothing happened.
Henry flapped and flapped.

He tried harder, and then

his feet left the ground.
Henry loved to fly.

Henry, with his large beak,
two long legs,
beautiful feathers,
and strong wings,
could do something special.

And Henry loved to share it.